This Is Matter:
Solids, Liquids, and Gases

by Rebecca Matos

Table of Contents

Introduction

Look at this book. The book is **matter**.

Look at this lake. The lake is matter. Read this book. You will learn about matter.

▲ The lake is matter.

▲ Look at this cloud. The cloud is matter.

See the Glossary on page 22.

What Is Matter?

Everything is matter. **Solids** are matter.

▲ This rock is a solid. The rock is matter.

Liquids are matter. **Gases** are matter, too.

▲ Gases are in the air around us. The air is matter.

▲ This water is a liquid. The water is matter.

Chapter 1

Matter occupies space. This building occupies space.

Matter has **mass**. This train has mass.

It's a Fact

Mass is the amount of matter something has.

▲ This train is matter.

What Are Solids?

Solids are matter. Solids have **shape**. Solids have **volume**.

It's a Fact

Volume is how much space something occupies.

▲ This elephant has shape. This elephant has volume. This elephant is a solid.

Some solids are hard. Some solids are soft.

▲ This bread is a solid.
This bread is soft.

Try This

1. Find solids that are soft.
2. Make a list.
3. Find solids that are hard.
4. Make a list.

▲ This bridge is a solid. This bridge is hard.

How can you change a solid? You can cut a solid.

▲ The tree is a solid. This man cuts the tree.

You can bend a solid.

▲ The clay is a solid. This girl bends the clay.

You can heat a solid.

▲ The eggs are solids. You can heat eggs in a pan.

What Are Liquids?

Liquids are matter. Liquids have volume.

The swimming pool water is a liquid. The swimming pool water has volume.

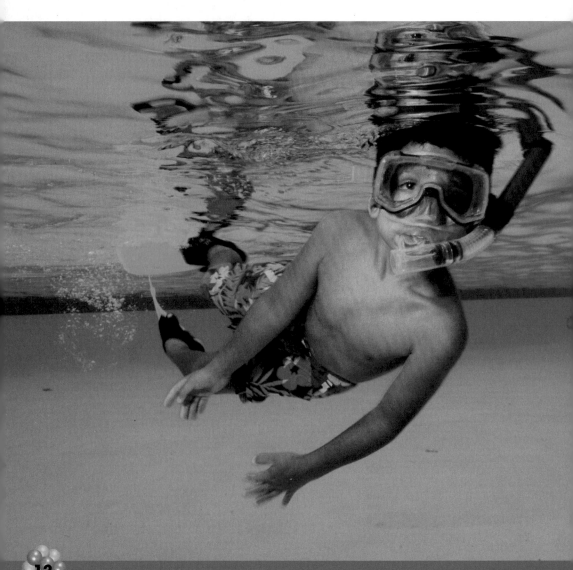

▲ This water is a liquid.

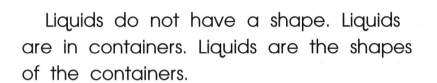

Liquids do not have a shape. Liquids are in containers. Liquids are the shapes of the containers.

Try This

You can see how liquids change shapes.

1. Get a tall, thin glass.
2. Pour in one cup of water.
3. Get a short, wide glass.
4. Pour in one cup of water.

Did You Know?

Rain is a liquid.
Rain is not in a container.

Chapter 3

There are many kinds of liquids. Some liquids flow quickly.

▲ This water flows quickly.

▲ This milk flows quickly.

Some liquids flow slowly.

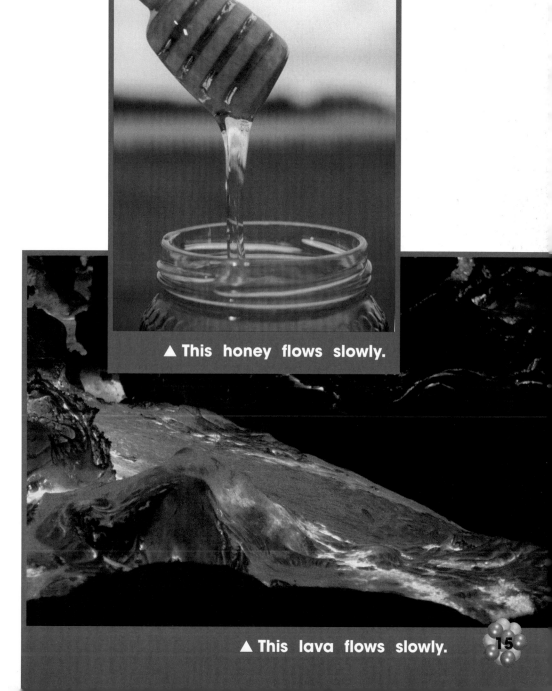

▲ This honey flows slowly.

▲ This lava flows slowly.

What Are Gases?

Gases are matter. Gases do not have shape.

▲ Air filled this balloon.

Gases fill the space they are in. Gases spread out in a large space. Gases squeeze together in a small space.

▲ Air filled these balloons.

Water vapor is gas. Water vapor happens when water boils.

▲ Boiling water makes water vapor.

Gases are all around you. You cannot see most gases.

▲ The air you breathe is a gas.

Summary

Everything is matter. Solids are matter. Liquids are matter. Gases are matter.

What Is Matter?

occupies space
has mass

What Are Solids?

matter

have shape

have volume

hard or soft

can change shape

What Are Liquids?

matter

do not have shape

have volume

in containers

flow quickly or slowly

What Are Gases?

matter
do not have shape
fill the space they are in
water vapor
all around us

Think About It

1. What are solids?
2. How are solids and liquids alike?
3. How are solids and gases different?

21

Glossary

gases matter with no shape

Gases are matter.

liquids matter with volume but no shape

Liquids can move and flow.

mass the amount of matter something has

*Matter has **mass**.*

matter everything; solids, liquids, or gases

Matter occupies space.

shape form

*Solids have **shape**.*

solids matter with shape and volume

*Some **solids** are hard.*

volume the amount of space something occupies

*Solids and liquids have **volume**.*

Index